SUPER
TRUCKS

Series Creator:

David Salariya was
born in Dundee, Scotland, where
he studied illustration and
printmaking. He has illustrated a
wide range of books and has
created many new series of books
for publishers in the UK and
overseas. In 1989 he established
The Salariya Book Company. He
lives in Brighton with his wife,
illustrator Shirley Willis, and
their son Jonathan.

Artist:

Nick Hewetson was
educated in Sussex at Brighton
Technical School and studied
illustration at Eastbourne
College of Art. He has since
illustrated a wide variety of
children's books.

Artist:

Mark Bergin was born
in Hastings in 1961. He studied
at Eastbourne College of Art and
has specialized in historical
reconstructions, aviation, and
maritime subjects since 1983.
He has been commissioned by
aerospace companies and has
illustrated a number of books
on flight. He has illustrated
many books in the prize-winning
Inside Story series as well as
Space Shuttle, **Wonders of the
World**, and **Castle** in the *Fast
Forward* series.

Author:

Ian Graham was born
in Belfast in 1953. He studied
applied physics at The City
University, London, and took
a postgraduate diploma in
journalism at the same
university, specializing in
science and technology
journalism. After four years
as an editor of consumer
electronics magazines, he
became a freelance author and
journalist. Since then, he has
written more than one hundred
children's non-fiction books and
numerous magazine articles.

Editor:

Karen Barker Smith

Editorial Assistant:

Stephanie Cole

Created, designed, and produced by
THE SALARIYA BOOK COMPANY LTD
25 Marlborough Place, Brighton BN1 1UB

Repro by Modern Age.

Printed in Hong Kong

ISBN 0-531-14618-9 (Lib. Bdg.)
ISBN 0-531-14810-6 (Pbk.)

First American edition 2001 by Franklin Watts
Grolier Publishing Co.,Inc.
90 Sherman Turnpike
Danbury, CT 06816

Visit Franklin Watts on the Internet at:
http://publishing.grolier.com

A catalog record for this title is available from
the Library of Congress.

SUPER TRUCKS

Written by
IAN GRAHAM

Illustrated by
MARK BERGIN
and
NICK HEWETSON

Created and designed by
DAVID SALARIYA

W
FRANKLIN WATTS
A Division of Grolier Publishing
NEW YORK • LONDON • HONG KONG • SYDNEY
DANBURY, CONNECTICUT

Contents

The First Trucks

1898 Daimler

The first self-propelled trucks were steam-powered monsters. They were heavy and slow with engines that belched black smoke. Before they could start, the driver had to light the boiler and heat a tank of water to produce a head of steam. Motor trucks, which were first produced in Germany in the 1890s, were a great improvement. They were ready to go as soon as their gasoline engines were started. However, most freight was still hauled by horse-drawn wagons and steam locomotives, until trucks proved their usefulness during World War I (1914–18). The thousands of military trucks left over after the war started a new road haulage industry in Europe and the United States in the 1920s. Manufacturers started making new vehicles specially designed to carry freight. Driver comfort was not a high priority in these early trucks. The cab was often open to the weather, and solid rubber tires gave a bumpy, uncomfortable ride.

German engineer Gottlieb Daimler built the first motor truck in 1896. It had a four-horsepower engine. Like the 1898 model shown above, it was little more than a motorized platform with a seat, but it was the latest thing in truck technology at the time.

Autocar 2 Tons

The Autocar 2 Tons (left) was introduced in 1926. Early models had an open cab, with only a short roof to cover the driver. "2 Tons" referred to the weight the truck could carry. The truck itself weighed 7-10 tons, depending on the model (there were 20 versions). Autocar is one of the oldest U.S. truck manufacturers. It began in 1897 as the Pittsburgh Motor Car Company.

1911 British Lacre

LC 1676

1926 Chevrolet

By the 1920s, trucks like this 1926 Chevrolet 1-tonner (above) were looking less like horseless carriages and more like special-purpose motor trucks.

1931 Chevrolet

J 5819

Early trucks like this British Lacre (above), dating from 1911, owed a lot to the design of horse-drawn carriages. They had wooden wheels with solid rubber tires. Lighting was provided by oil or gas lamps. The driver's cab, though simple, often had ornately carved wooden trim.

This 1931 Chevrolet truck (right) is fitted with metal wheels and pneumatic tires. Pneumatic tires lasted four times longer than solid tires and also helped cushion the vehicle from lumps and bumps in the road. This truck had an enclosed cab to protect the driver from the weather.

Early trucks spent much more time off the road than modern vehicles, because they had to be loaded and unloaded by hand.

Trucks for Tasks

Trucks are vehicles used to carry freight by road. The shape and size of every truck are determined by the task it is intended for. The design begins with the chassis, the main frame on which the rest of the truck is built. The chassis is made from steel beams welded into the shape of a ladder running the length of the truck. Some of the smallest trucks, or vans, are no bigger than cars and use the same type of gasoline engine as cars. Most trucks are powered by diesel engines because they are simpler, stronger, more reliable, and less expensive to operate than gasoline engines. The number of wheels a truck has depends on the weight it will have to carry. Heavier trucks need more wheels to spread their weight evenly over the road. Some types of trucks are equipped with machinery, such as a winch to pull things onboard or a hoist to lift things on and off. Most trucks are able to carry a variety of different sorts of freight, but some trucks are specialized to do one particular task. Trucks designed for special tasks include fire engines, military transporters, concrete trucks, refrigerated food transporters, tow trucks, and road cranes.

Recovery trucks have a rear platform that tilts down to the ground (right). A car can then be winched up onto the platform, which then tips up level again. Like tow trucks, these recovery vehicles are used to collect broken-down cars and remove illegally parked or abandoned vehicles.

Tankers transport all sorts of liquids. They deliver gasoline to fuel stations and a variety of liquid chemicals to manufacturers.

Trucks can haul even larger loads by towing trailers behind them. A truck-plus-trailer is called a drawbar-trailer outfit.

Tow trucks collect vehicles that have broken down or been involved in accidents. They tow them away by using a winch mounted on the rear of the vehicle.

Winch

Airport tugs, or tractors, are strange-looking vehicles used to move aircraft. Most of the vehicle is taken up by its powerful diesel engine, with a small driver's cab at the front. Tugs are built very low and flat so that they can fit underneath an airplane's nose and hook up to its nose wheel to tow it.

Recovery truck

Rigid truck (viewed from below)

All trucks are either rigid or articulated. Rigid trucks (above) are built on a single frame, or chassis. The cab is permanently connected to the rest of the vehicle. Articulated trucks (left) swivel behind the cab and engine, which together form a unit called the tractor.

Articulated truck (viewed from below)

Heavy trucks transport large loads long distances between cities. The largest of these vehicles can weigh over 40 tons.

Delivery trucks are smaller than heavy trucks and better suited to carrying smaller loads over shorter distances.

Tipper trucks transport loose materials such as gravel and rock for the construction industry. The back of the truck tips up to empty the load out.

Truck Racing

Trucks are the most unlikely racing vehicles. They are designed to carry equipment, make deliveries, or haul heavy loads, not to race. However, truck racing is very popular. All sorts of trucks are raced, from open-back pick-up trucks to articulated truck tractor units. Today's racing trucks are specially built, with racing engines designed and tuned for high-speed maneuvering on the track. These engines make racing trucks as powerful as many racing cars.

Racing cars and their teams are transported to and from racetracks in giant trailers (below). They house the car, a workshop compartment, and living quarters for the team — a kitchen, lounge, and shower, sometimes a bedroom too.

A super truck based on a Leyland Landtrain rears up into a wheelie (above).

Monster trucks like *BigFoot* (above) compete at truck events. They try to outdo each other in events including doing wheelies and climbing over obstacles.

The NASCAR Craftsman Truck races draw large crowds. Below, a Craftsman Series super truck.

A group of 700-horsepower racing trucks make a dash for the first corner (right). Drivers say the latest racing trucks handle in a surprisingly similar way to racing cars. The main difference is that the truck bodies create less downward pull to help them grip the track.

Freightliner Defiance (left) is a dragster truck. It is powered by a 1930s fighter-plane engine built on a truck chassis. The 28-litre V12 Allison piston engine, burning aviation fuel, gives the truck a top speed of 168 mph (270 kph). The rear wing helps pull the vehicle down onto the track.

International Endeavor III (above) is a unique truck designed to set speed records. Its diesel engine runs at 2,500 horsepower, compared to less than 500 horsepower for a normal road truck. *International Endeavor III* has reached a speed of 224 mph (360 kph) on the Bonneville Salt Flats in Utah. To slow down from such a high speed, it has to use parachutes.

Construction Trucks

The construction industry depends on heavy trucks to move enormous quantities of materials to and from construction sites. Whatever the type of structure being built, from homes and skyscrapers to roads and bridges, large volumes of concrete are always needed, so concrete-mixer trucks are frequent visitors to construction sites. Vehicles that spend most of their time on rough or loose ground are sometimes fitted with low-pressure tires that hug the ground better. Dump trucks are often used to move materials around construction sites. These small trucks have a large bucket for carrying materials and are very maneuverable. Some are jointed in the middle so they can turn into the tightest of spaces.

Road crane

A truck chassis can have a range of bodies and machinery built on it. One specialized type of truck is the road crane. The crane is made from a series of sections that slide inside each other for easy transport. There is one cab for driving the vehicle and another for operating the crane.

Articulated Trucks

The largest trucks are articulated, which means they have a swivel joint behind the driver's cab. The joint lets the truck maneuver more easily than a rigid truck of the same size. The rear part of the truck, where the freight is carried, can also be disconnected and replaced within minutes by a different load. The back of the truck is called a semitrailer, because it has no road wheels at the front. The front of the semitrailer rests on the back of the tractor unit. When a semitrailer has to be unhitched from its tractor, small temporary wheels are lowered to hold it up.

Streamlined roof

Airflow

Half of the energy generated by a truck's engine is wasted by overcoming air resistance. One way of cutting air resistance is to fit a taller, smoothly streamlined roof to the cab to deflect air around the load.

Semitrailer

Air filter

Curved vanes

Cutaway of a concrete mixer

Construction Trucks

The construction industry depends on heavy trucks to move enormous quantities of materials to and from construction sites. Whatever the type of structure being built, from homes and skyscrapers to roads and bridges, large volumes of concrete are always needed, so concrete-mixer trucks are frequent visitors to construction sites. Vehicles that spend most of their time on rough or loose ground are sometimes fitted with low-pressure tires that hug the ground better. Dump trucks are often used to move materials around construction sites. These small trucks have a large bucket for carrying materials and are very maneuverable. Some are jointed in the middle so they can turn into the tightest of spaces.

A concrete mixer's drum has curved vanes inside it (above). When the drum revolves in one direction, the vanes mix the concrete by keeping it moving and stopping it from setting. When the mixer arrives at the site, the drum is turned in the opposite direction (below). The vanes feed the concrete out the end of the drum and down a delivery chute.

Road crane

A truck chassis can have a range of bodies and machinery built on it. One specialized type of truck is the road crane. The crane is made from a series of sections that slide inside each other for easy transport. There is one cab for driving the vehicle and another for operating the crane.

13

Articulated Trucks

Streamlined roof

Airflow

Half of the energy generated by a truck's engine is wasted by overcoming air resistance. One way of cutting air resistance is to fit a taller, smoothly streamlined roof to the cab to deflect air around the load.

The largest trucks are articulated, which means they have a swivel joint behind the driver's cab. The joint lets the truck maneuver more easily than a rigid truck of the same size. The rear part of the truck, where the freight is carried, can also be disconnected and replaced within minutes by a different load. The back of the truck is called a semitrailer, because it has no road wheels at the front. The front of the semitrailer rests on the back of the tractor unit. When a semitrailer has to be unhitched from its tractor, small temporary wheels are lowered to hold it up.

Semitrailer

Air filter

Cabou...

In-line layout

Hinged hood

Exhaust pipe

Trunnion plate

The in-line layout truck design is most popular in the United States, where there is more room on the highways for long-nose models. The biggest advantage of the in-line layout (above and below) is that the engine is easy to get to for repairs and servicing. The whole engine cover, or hood, hinges up and forward (above). To save weight, the hood is often made from fiberglass, which is lighter than metal but just as strong. U.S. trucks often gleam with polished chrome work. The tall vertical exhaust pipes, drum-shaped air filter, and radiator grille at the front are often finished in chrome.

Radiator grille

Engine hood

...t between an articulated truck's tractor and ...iler is called the fifth wheel. A tractor is hitched ...semitrailer by backing up to it. The semitrailer ...onto a plate called a trunnion plate, fitted to ...t of the tractor (above). As the tractor continues ...se, a pin pointing down from the front of the ...ler drops into a hole in the middle of the plate, ...the two parts of the vehicle together. Finally, the ...ler's temporary front wheels are raised.

...eels — steering

Green wheels — steering

4 x 2

4 x 4

6 x 2

Yellow wheels — neither steering nor driven

6 x 4

Most family cars have two axles with a wheel on each end. One of the axles is driven (or controlled) by the engine. Trucks have more axles, and more than one of them may be driven. A truck with two axles, one driven, is described as a 4 x 2, which means it has four wheels, two of which are driven.

6 x 6

8 x 4

15

...heels — driven

17

Tippers and Lifters

Tipper trucks and dump trucks carry heavy loads of loose material, which they unload by tipping up the back of their trucks. Tippers transport their loads by road, while dumpers move materials around at construction sites. The back of the truck is raised by one or more hydraulic rams. A hydraulic ram is a piston that is forced through a tube by oil pressure, powered by the truck's engine. Longer rams are made from several pistons that slide inside each other. Hydraulic rams are also the mechanical muscles that power a variety of other lifting devices used by trucks.

Skip truck

Hydraulic arm

Skip

A skip truck (above) has two hydraulic arms at the back for loading and unloading skips — metal containers for transporting garbage and other materials.

Forklift truck

This modern version of the traditional forklift truck (above) can raise and lower a load like a normal forklift, and it can also reach its arm forward to place loads onto shelves.

The Terex Titan (below) is the world's biggest dump truck. It works at mines and quarries, where it can transport up to 550 tons of rubble or mineral ore at a time.

1927 Autocar
tipper truck

Garbage truck

*Levers powered
by the engine*

The tipping mechanism of early tipper trucks, like the 1927 Autocar model (above), was operated by levers powered by the vehicle's small 20 or 30 horsepower engine. A modern tipper (below) is raised by a hydraulic ram that can call on an engine of 200 to 500 horsepower, sometimes more, to tip greater loads. The cabs of trucks like tippers are basic compared to the cabs of long-distance trucks.

Garbage trucks (above) have a compactor to squash collected garbage into a smaller space. The garbage is thrown into an open hopper at the back of the truck (right). When the hopper is full, the compactor is used. A heavy metal panel swings up over the garbage, crushes it, and scoops it forward into the truck.

Hydraulic ram

Hopper

Hopper

Garbage

Compactor

1

2

4

The hopper is filled with garbage (1). The compactor swings out over the garbage (2), moves down behind it (3), and scoops it out of the hopper into the truck (4).

World War I truck

Military Trucks

Military trucks are essential for transporting soldiers and equipment. They have to be particularly rugged and reliable, as well as easy to repair and maintain. Many military trucks are adapted from civilian models and strengthened especially for military service. Several different types of military vehicles can be built from the same basic chassis. One model might be a general transport truck, another might be a fuel tanker, and another might have a crane on the back. In addition to general transport work, military trucks also have to carry troops, tow equipment, and sometimes carry weapons. All-terrain models have a high ground clearance (the space under the truck) to protect the underside of the vehicle from damage on rough ground. Trucks intended to operate in combat zones have to be armor-plated for extra protection.

Military trucks such as the one above were used in large numbers for the first time during World War I (1914–18). They frequently broke down and their thin wheels sank into the mud, but they still managed to prove their usefulness as military transporters.

The six-wheel General Motors GMC CCKW 353 (right) is one of the best-known American military trucks. More than half a million were made after 1941. It was a rugged and reliable truck that remained in service for decades.

GMC CCKW 353

Tank transporter   *Battle tank*

Battle tanks are transported by road on tank transporters (above). These powerful vehicles spread the immense weight of a tank (30 to 65 tons) over a greater area to prevent damage to the road surface. They also burn less fuel and move faster than the tank.

An army road-crane, the military version of the Swedish Scania P113 HK, rescues a vehicle that has run into trouble (right). In addition to the crane, it has a winch. All three of the truck's axles are driven by the vehicle's 11-litre, 380-horsepower engine to give better grip. The engine is modular, meaning that it is built from a simple set of parts that are easy to replace if a repair is needed. The ring on the roof of the cab is for mounting a machine gun.

An AM General M923 5-ton truck (right) tows a howitzer (a type of gun). This truck lets the driver alter the tire pressure from inside the cab. Lowering the pressure makes the tires softer and better able to grip soft ground.

AM General M923

Howitzer

Military breakdown crane

Caterpillar tracks

Machine gun mount

Scania P113 HK

A military crane lifts out a tank's engine and lowers a replacement into position (above). The crane is fitted with caterpillar tracks instead of wheels, to stop it from sinking into soft ground. Each track is an endless chain of links that spreads the vehicle's weight.

SCANIA

113н 310

65416

Fire Engines

Modern fire engines can be traced back to the first fire engines built in Britain in the 17th century. These early machines were simply hand-operated water-pumps mounted on wheels. Modern fire engines are much more advanced, multifunction vehicles. More complex than ordinary trucks, they carry firefighters into action and provide pumping power for water-jets and other equipment such as hydraulic ladders and elevator platforms. They also carry the equipment necessary to fight fires and carry out a variety of rescue operations. If extra equipment is needed, it can be brought to the scene by emergency trucks called rescue tenders.

This 1903 Merryweather Fire King (above) was driven by a steam engine, which also powered the water pump. It could pump about 475 gallons (1,800 liters) of water every minute.

Merryweather made some of the earliest fire engines in Britain to have gasoline engines. This 1903 model with a hose reel and wheeled escape ladder served in London (below).

Water hydrant

This 1952 Crown Firecoach (below) is a classic American fire engine. Its pumps were able to supply water at the rate of 345 gallons (1,300 liters) per minute.

When fire engines arrive at the scene of a fire, firefighters connect hoses between the trucks and the nearest water outlets or hydrants. A second set of hoses is run out from the trucks to the firefighting positions. A major fire may be attacked from several points on the ground and also from above, by firefighters on ladders and elevated platforms. The engines take water from the hydrants and pump it through to the firefighters at high pressure. Their engines must work reliably to keep the hoses supplied with water.

Remote
as Darw
Austral
coast, c
deliveri
by road
ports su
in the s

Monitor

6 26

orts worldwide have their own
scue services (above). Since
s may involve aviation fuel,
trucks spray foam instead of
directional nozzles called
n top of the trucks.

raulic ladder (right) is
ed on a rotating base
ntable, so that it can
ned and raised in
rection.

Water jet

CROWN
9

1952 Crown Firecoach

Metal feet

Before a hydraulic ladder or elevator platform is raised from a fire engine, metal feet are extended from each side of the vehicle (above). They give the truck a wider, firmer base to hold it steady so that it is not pulled over by the weight of the ladder or platform.

Trucks to Come

Designs for future trucks are being shaped by two main factors: the need to cut costs and reduce air pollution. Making a truck more slick and streamlined lets it slip through the air more easily, so it wastes less fuel overcoming air resistance. When a vehicle burns less fuel, it is less expensive to operate and it reduces air pollution. Switching to cleaner fuels is an even better way to reduce pollution. Hydrogen is the cleanest fuel of all. When hydrogen is burned, it combines with oxygen in the air to make nothing more harmful than water vapor. From time to time, truck manufacturers produce prototypes of new trucks to act as showcases for new technology. These prototypes are also called concept trucks. Most of them will never go into production, but they are useful for trying out new ideas and testing people's reactions to them.

Prototype for multi-drop delivery truck

The DAF XFC (Xtreme Future Concept) has a wedge-shaped cab (below). This aerodynamic shape slips through the air more easily than a standard cab. It is also said to be safer — a vehicle hitting the cab is pushed to the side.

Volvo's ECT (Environmental Concept Truck) (right) was designed to show how much kinder trucks could be to the environment. The ECT reduces air pollution in cities by using a gas turbine engine instead of diesel. The gas turbine powers a generator, which makes electricity for a set of electric motors that drive the wheels. The gas turbine engine has much cleaner exhaust emissions than the diesel engines that most trucks are powered by today.

DAF XFC

Volvo ECT

Internet shopping is creating a growing need for a new generation of stop-start multi-drop delivery trucks. This prototype (left), produced by B-Style Automotive for the Dutch Ministry of Transport and Communications, is one answer. It has a walk-through cab and load box to make it easier for the driver to pick out packages and get in and out of the truck. It can carry a load of 4.5 tons, and its 0.6-gal (2.3-liter) LPG (Liquid Petroleum Gas) engine is far kinder to the environment than a diesel engine.

In the future, trucks may pull up at natural gas pumps (above) to fill up, instead of diesel oil pumps. Natural gas, which is made mostly from methane, is the cleanest of all the fossil fuels. And because it is a gas, it mixes easily with air inside the engine and burns very efficiently.

Electric motors

Generator

Fuel cell

Gas turbine engine

Some future trucks might not burn fuel inside an engine at all. Instead, they may be driven by electric motors powered by devices called fuel cells (right). Fuel cells work like batteries except that they do not run down or need recharging. They take in hydrogen and make it react chemically with oxygen from the air, producing electricity and water vapor.

Glossary

Aerodynamic
Able to move easily through air.

Aviation fuel
Fuel used to power airplanes.

Axle
A rod that passes through the center of a wheel.

Caterpillar tracks
A series of metal plates linked together and fitted over a vehicle's wheels.

Chrome work
Parts of a vehicle coated with chromium, a silver-coated metal.

Cylinder
One of the metal tubes inside an engine, where the fuel is burned.

Diesel
A type of engine, invented by German engineer Rudolf Diesel.

Dragster
A powerful racing vehicle designed to accelerate as fast as possible down a track 1,312 ft (400 m) long.

Fiberglass
A material made from woven glass fibers embedded in plastic.

Fossil fuels
Natural fuels, such as coal and gas, which were formed millions of years ago from the remains of living organisms.

Freight
The goods carried by different forms of transport.

Gas turbine engine
A type of engine that burns fuel to produce gas, which spins a turbine (a finned wheel that is turned as gas rushes past it and pushes against the fins).

Haulage industry
An industry that makes money from the transport of goods.

Hoist
A lifting device or machine.

Horsepower
A measure of how fast an engine converts the energy in its fuel into movement energy.

Hydrant
A pipe in the street that is attached to the main water supply so that water can be drawn from it through a hose.

Hydraulic
Operated by pressurized fluid.

Hydrogen
A colorless, odorless, and tasteless gas.

Locomotives
Engines that pull railway carriages and freight wagons.

Pneumatic
Air-filled.

Prototype
The first, or original, model of a vehicle used to test its design before it goes into production.

Tractor
A vehicle used to pull heavy loads, such as the cab and engine units that pull articulated trucks.

Winch
A motor-driven drum used to lift things by winding rope or cable around the drum.

Super Truck Facts

The biggest transport vehicles ever built are the two crawler transporters that carried the Apollo/Saturn 5 moon-landing rockets to the launchpad in the 1960s and 1970s. They are now used to carry the space shuttle and its mobile launch platform to the launchpad.

Tires for the world's biggest dump trucks can weigh up to 5.6 tons each and stand more than 11 ft (3.5 m) high.

Trucks can have up to eighteen forward gears and two reverse gears, compared to five forward gears and one reverse for a family car.

Truck drivers spend so much time at the wheel that their seats have their own suspension systems to make them more comfortable to sit in for long periods.

On long journeys, a truck driver may have to be away from home overnight. Some cabs are fitted with bunks to sleep in and even a refrigerator, coffee machine, and microwave oven for preparing meals.

The latest trucks have onboard computers that keep the driver fully informed about the state of the truck's engine. If a problem develops, the onboard computer can give details of what has gone wrong.

Truck drivers can be connected to their base by satellite radio. This means that the truck's position can be pinpointed at any time.

The longest truck in the world is 570 ft (174 m) long and is called Le Tourneau Arctic Snow Train. It was built for the U.S. army to use in arctic regions.

Amphibious trucks are able to drive both across land and through water.

It is quite normal for a truck driver to cover about 100,000 miles (170,000 km) in a year.

During World War I (1914–1918), the number of transport vehicles near the front line in France increased from 6,000 to 92,000.

Chronology

1769 French military engineer Nicolas Cugnot builds the first self-propelled vehicle, a steam tractor that can travel at 2.2 mph (3.6 kph).

1784 Scotsman William Murdock builds a working model of a steam-powered carriage.

1789 Oliver Evans is granted the first American patent for a steam-powered land vehicle.

1801 English engineer Richard Trevithick builds a steam-powered carriage.

1815 Scottish engineer John McAdam invents a new road surface called tarmacadam made from crushed rock and tar.

1831 A steam-powered ten-seat bus starts a passenger service between London and Stratford.

1845 Scotsman Robert William Thomson invents the rubber tire.

1858 The first successful steam-powered fire engine is introduced.

1863 Jean-Joseph-Etienne Lenoir builds the first vehicle powered by an internal combustion engine instead of a steam engine.

1885 Karl Benz builds a three-wheel automobile powered by an internal combustion engine that burns gasoline fuel.

1887 Gottlieb Daimler builds a four-wheel automobile powered by an internal combustion engine.

1888 Scotsman John Boyd Dunlop invents the pneumatic (air-filled) rubber tire.

1891 French engineers Andre and Edouard Michelin invent an inflatable tire that can be removed from the wheel rim and replaced by another tire.

1892 French engineer Rudolf

Diesel invents a new type of engine, the diesel engine, which will later power trucks and other commercial vehicles.

1895 The Benz company builds a gasoline-fueled bus.

1902 Drum brakes and disc brakes, the two types of brakes used by modern trucks, are invented.

1903 The first gasoline-fueled fire engine is introduced.

1908 The first twin wheels for trucks are introduced. A twin wheel is two wheels on the same axle where there was only one before.

1913 The removable steel wheel is introduced. Trucks begin to carry spare wheels.

1914 An American automobile repair man, Ernest Holmes, designs the world's first tow truck.

1915 Detroit blacksmith August Fruehauf invents the tractor trailer, a truck with a separate driver's cab and trailer.

1916 4,500 trucks, buses, and ambulances help transport four million French troops to defend Verdun in France during World War I.

1917 The French army uses a specially built fleet of trucks to transport carrier pigeons. Each truck holds eighty birds in nineteen cages. The birds are used to carry messages tied to their legs.

1921 The first motorway is built, in Germany.

1925 The Michelin company develops a low-pressure heavy-goods vehicle tire.

1930 English engineer Bernard Dicksee builds a diesel engine that

can be used by road vehicles. The 2.1-gal (8.1-litre), six-cylinder engine is fitted in trucks.

1939 The first vehicles with automatic clutches, to make gear changing faster and easier, are introduced.

1941 The first Jeep, a general purpose military vehicle, is introduced.

1947 The Goodyear company introduces the tubeless tire.

1951 Power steering is introduced by Chrysler.

1954 The size of containers, used for transporting freight on trucks, is standardized.

1982 The first truck diesel emission regulations come into force in Britain.

1983 The gross weight of trucks allowed by law on British roads is increased from 32 tons to 38 tons.

1996 Ron Hornaday wins his second U.S. NASCAR Craftsman Truck Series championship.

1997 A dragster truck called *Joint Venture*, based on a Freightliner FLD120 truck, sets a speed record of 225.5 mph (362.9 kph) on the Bonneville Salt Flats in Utah.

1998 Ron Hornaday wins his second U.S. NASCAR Craftsman Truck Series championship.

1999 Jack Sprague wins the U.S. NASCAR Craftsman Truck Series championship for the second time.

Index